Enrich your Grammar

Primary 1

by
Anuradha Verma
M.A., B.Ed.
(Delhi University)

Edited by
Reita Sharma M.A., B.Ed.
Ex Teacher
Delhi Public School, Dhanbad

Edited by
Vimla Kaul M.A.
Ex Teacher
Carmel Convent, Dhanbad

Reviewed by
HS Bhatia
Ex Sr Lecturer (English)
AS College, Khanna
(Punjab University)

Name : ______________________

Class : ______________________

School : ______________________

the Bookmaster
DS Publishers India

Published by
DS Publishers India
7/7 Ansari Road
Daryaganj
New Delhi 110 002
INDIA
+91 (11) 4156 3757
info@dspublishers.com

25th Impression 2025

9788187131717

Typesetting by
Lovika Arts

Cover Design by
White Mice Media

Printed in India at
Balaji Offset

₹195

PREFACE

The utility of grammar is to learn the correct way to gain expertise in a language, both written and spoken. But the conventional method of teaching and learning has long since become obsolete. In the modern method, advocated by educationists the world over, the integrated approach has been adopted. Thus, it is felt that the best way to learn a language is to use it.

The contextualised method wherein the learner learns to use the language correctly through language activities involving the skills like speaking, listening, reading and writing, is the premise on which this series has been designed. It concentrates on the usage of correct language and improving the learners' command of the English language through group work and other communicative activities.

In places where the need for focus lessons is felt to clarify, reinforce and consolidate the usage, detailed explanations have been given for better understanding.

The lessons encourage self-help to breed familiarity with the language.

Constructive suggestions are solicited.

CONTENTS

Unit 1	Sentences	5
Unit 2	Nouns	7
Unit 3	Nouns - Singular and Plural (1)	18
Unit 4	Nouns - Singular and Plural (2)	24
Unit 5	Nouns - Gender	32
Unit 6	Pronouns	39
Unit 7	Verbs	44
Unit 8	The Verb – 'To Be'	51
Unit 9	The Verb – 'To Have'	56
Unit 10	The Verb – 'To Do'	61
Unit 11	Tenses	68
Unit 12	Adjectives	74
Unit 13	Common Vocabulary	82
Unit 14	Reading Skills	91
	Answers	100

UNIT 1

SENTENCES

A group of words which makes a complete **sense** is a **sentence**.

A sentence begins with a **Capital Letter**.

A sentence is a complete **thought**.

Example

–She loves to eat.

This is a complete thought. It is a sentence.

Only **loves to eat** is not a complete thought.

It is not a sentence.

Exercise 1

Put a (✓) against the sentences.

1. He is two years old. ☐
2. a dark night. ☐
3. Stars twinkle. ☐
4. She is a nurse. ☐

5. The boys are flying kites. ☐

6. with her doll. ☐

7. He has two sisters. ☐

8. A lion lives in a den. ☐

9. eats ice-cream. ☐

Exercise 2

Match the words on the left with their correct pairs on the right to make a complete sentence.

1. The little boy	•	•	throughout the day.
2. It rained	•	•	played with her doll.
3. The class was	•	•	fond of chocolates.
4. The little girl	•	•	rode his bicycle.
5. John is	•	•	the first prize.
6. Mary loves to	•	•	over by nine o'clock.
7. The girl won	•	•	eat ice-cream.

UNIT 2

NOUNS

Nouns are the **names** of persons, places, animals, birds and things.

Example

teacher, nurse, barber, man — *names of* ***persons***.

lion, tiger, cat, monkey — *names of* ***animals***.

library, stadium, school, garden — *names of* ***places***.

pencil, umbrella, coat, dress — *names of* ***things***.

Exercise 1

Can you name these pictures? Write their names in the given boxes.

1.

2.

3.

4.

5.

6.

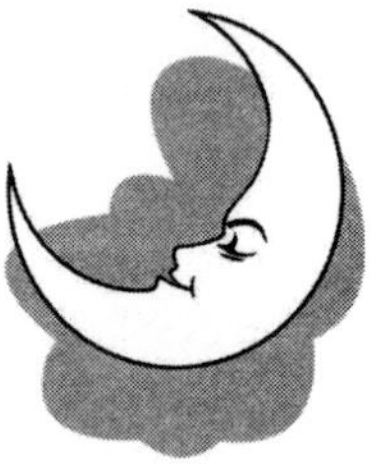

7.

8.

9.

10.

Exercise 2

From the list of words given below pick out the names of persons, places, animals and things.

church	dog	clothes	tiger
car	cat	Taj Mahal	island
girl	man	policeman	London
water	cow	hospital	flower
Diana	baby	leaf	bear

Persons	**Places**	**Animals**	**Things**
______	______	______	______
______	______	______	______
______	______	______	______
______	______	______	______
______	______	______	______

Exercise 3

A. *Write the names of 6* **persons** *you know.*

1. ____________________ 2. ____________________

3. ____________________ 4. ____________________

5. ____________________ 6. ____________________

B. *Write the names of 6* **places** *you like to visit.*

1. ____________________ 2. ____________________

3. ____________________ 4. ____________________

5. ____________________ 6. ____________________

C. *Write the names of 6* **animals** *and* **birds**.

1. ____________________ 2. ____________________

3. ____________________ 4. ____________________

5. ____________________ 6. ____________________

D. *Write the names of 6 **things** in your school bag.*

1. ______________________ 2. ______________________

3. ______________________ 4. ______________________

5. ______________________ 6. ______________________

E. *Write the names of your 6 **friends**.*

1. ______________________ 2. ______________________

3. ______________________ 4. ______________________

5. ______________________ 6. ______________________

F. *Write the names of 6 **types** of **food** you like to eat.*

1. ______________________ 2. ______________________

3. ______________________ 4. ______________________

5. ______________________ 6. ______________________

Exercise 4

*Find out the **nouns** in the words given below. Circle them.*

Johnny	long	write	woman
happy	Paris	fat	book
rose	ribbon	run	read
go	kick	fast	mangoes
sky	star	twinkle	moon
stand	ugly	school	park
train	stop	hospital	fly

Exercise 5

Circle the **nouns** *in the following sentences.*

1. Lily has a new dress.
2. The horse lives in a stable.
3. The Nile is the longest river in the world.
4. Peter loves to play with balls.
5. The kind man helped the little boy.
6. Maria washes clothes every day.
7. Daisy reads the newspaper.
8. The students travel by bus.

Exercise 6

Underline the words which are ***not nouns***.

1.	book	animal	tiger	loves	jungle
2.	bird	peacock	brings	postman	toys
3.	stars	eat	moon	sky	night
4.	glass	picture	horse	sing	day
5.	children	teacher	sit	coffee	milk

Exercise 7

Make a list of all the ***nouns*** *that you see in the picture below.*

1. ____________________ 6. ____________________

2. ____________________ 7. ____________________

3. ____________________ 8. ____________________

4. ____________________ 9. ____________________

5. ____________________ 10. ____________________

Exercise 8

*Name the **persons** who do the things listed below. Choose from the table.*

Helping Words

washerman	*tailor*	*teacher*	*nurse*
barber	*postman*	*pilot*	*painter*
carpenter	*cobbler*	*milkman*	*grocer*

1. A ______________ is a person who makes clothes for us to wear.

2. A ______________ is a person who mends our shoes.

3. A ______________ is a person who teaches us.

4. A ______________ is a person who cuts our hair.

5. A ______________ is a person who brings our letters to our houses.

6. A ______________ is a person who washes our dirty clothes.

7. A ______________ is a person who looks after the sick people.

8. A ______________ is a person who paints our houses.

9. A ______________ is a person who makes things from wood.

10. A ______________ is a person who flies an aeroplane.

11. A ______________ is a person who sells rice, sugar, milk and cheese.

12. A ______________ is a person who brings us milk.

Exercise 9

Fill in the blanks with the help of the pictures given.

1. The ______________ is playing with a ball.

2. The ______________ is flying in the sky.

3. The ______________ is reading a book.

4. The ________________ is teaching in the class.

5. The ________________ are playing in the garden.

6. The ________________ is singing.

7. The ________________ is barking at the thief.

8. The ________________ is shining in the sky.

UNIT 3

NOUNS – SINGULAR & PLURAL (1)

The **noun** that means one person, one place or one thing is in the **singular** number.

Example

I have one **book**. 

My friend has one **bicycle**. 

Alice has one **apple**. 

John has a **car**. 

The **noun** that means more than one person, place or thing often ends in **s** or **es** is in the **plural** number.

Example

There are two **ducks** in the pond. 

Yesterday I had three **chocolates**. 

Alice has two **hens**. 

John has two **toy-trains**. 

Exercise 1

Look at the pictures. Then write the ***plurals*** *by adding 's'.*

1.

One car

Two ______________

2.

One dog

Three ______________

3.

One apple

Four ______________

4.

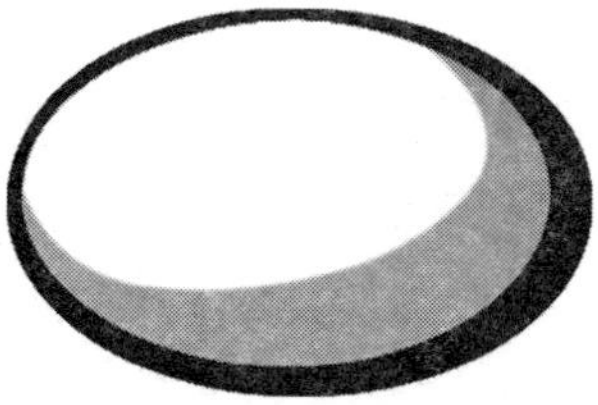

One egg

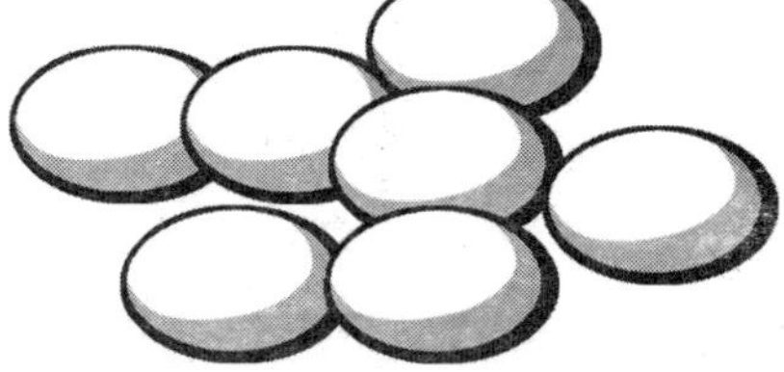

Many ______________

5.

One girl

Two ______________

6.

One white horse

Two white ______________

7.

One bottle

Three ______________

8.

One chair

Many ______________

9.

One little boy

Two little ______________

Exercise 2

Fill in the missing words.

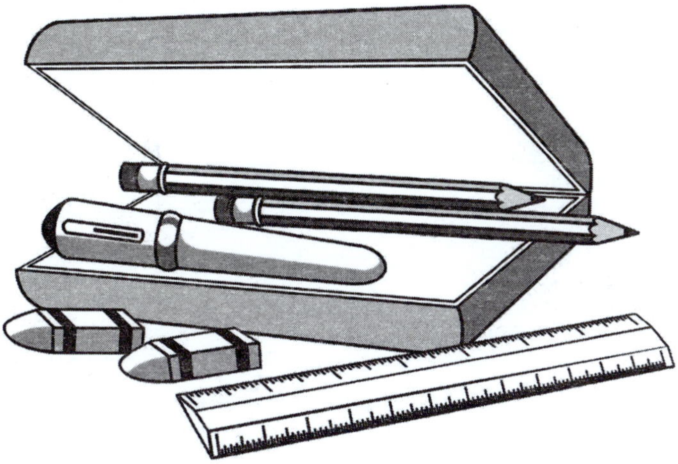

A. Look at Ruby's pencil box.

There are one ________________, two ________________,

one ________________ and two ________________.

B. Look at Miley's fruit basket.

She has three ________________, two ________________,

four ________________ and one ________________.

Exercise 3

How many birds are there in the bird park?

1. There are three ____________ swimming in the lake.
2. There are two ____________ on the bank of the lake.
3. There are two ____________ dancing in the ground.
4. There is one ____________ sitting on the branch of the tree.
5. There are four ____________ sitting on the wall.
6. There are two ____________ sitting in the tree.

Exercise 4

Fill in the blanks.

James has many toys.

1. 

He has two ____________ .

He has four ____________ .

2. 

He has one ____________ .

He also has three ____________.

3. 

He has two ____________ , but

he likes the ____________ best.

4. 

He has two ____________ .

His favourite is a ____________.

5. 

He has four ____________ , but

one is broken.

UNIT 4

NOUNS – SINGULAR & PLURAL (2)

Formation of the Plural

A. If a noun ends with the letter **y**, change **y** to **ies** to make it plural.

Example

cherr**y**

cherr**<u>ies</u>**

bab**y**

bab**<u>ies</u>**

Exercise 1

*Fill in the blanks with the **plurals**.*

1. one lady  two ____________ 
2. one berry  three ____________ 
3. one butterfly  four ____________ 
4. one candy  two ____________ 
5. one fly  many ____________ 

B. When a noun has a vowel (a, e, i, o, u) before it ends with the letter **y**, then just **s** is added to it.

Example

bo**y**

boy**s**

monke**y**

monkey**s**

Exercise 2

*Fill in the blanks with the **plurals** of the following.*

1. One day  two ______________ 

2. One ray  two ______________ 

3. One donkey  two ______________ 

4. One toy  two ______________ 

5. One tray 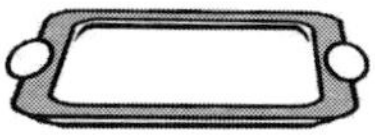 two ______________ 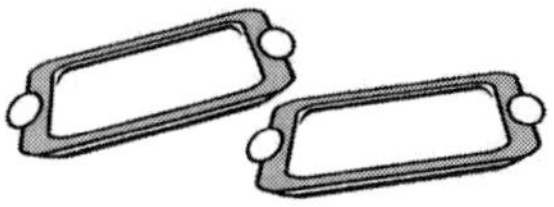

C. When a noun ends with **o**, then **es** is added to it.

Example

tomat**o**

tomato**es**

negr**o**

negro**es**

Exercise 3

*Fill in the blanks with the **plurals** of the following.*

1. one mango  two ______________ 
2. one buffalo  two ______________ 
3. one hero  two ______________ 
4. one potato  two ______________ 
5. one mosquito  two ______________ 

D. When a noun ends with **f** or **fe**, then **f** or **fe** is changed into **v** and **es** is added.

Example

lea**f**

lea**ves**

thie**f**

thie**ves**

Exercise 4

*Fill in the blanks with the **plurals** of the following.*

1. one life two ____________

2. one wife  two ____________ 

3. one calf  two ____________ 

E. There are a few nouns which form their plurals by changing the inside **vowel** of the singular.

Example

m**a**n

m**e**n

Exercise 5

Fill in the blanks with the ***plurals*** *of the following.*

1. one goose  two ____________ 

2. one woman  two ____________ 

3. one mouse  two ____________ 

4. one foot 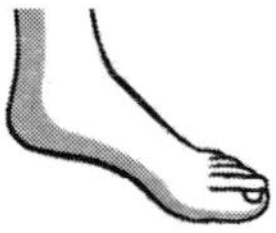 two ____________ 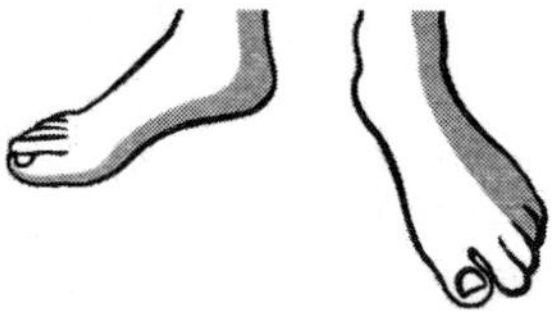

5. one tooth 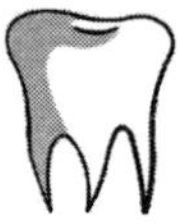 two ____________ 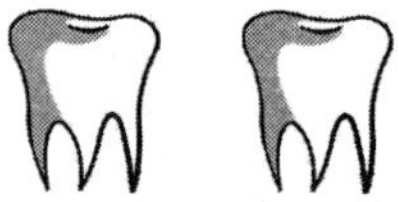

Exceptions

The following nouns end with **f** or **fe**. Only **s** is added to them to form their plurals.

Example

grief	grief**s**	chief	chief**s**
gulf	gulf**s**	brief	brief**s**
safe	safe**s**	proof	proof**s**
serf	serf**s**	strife	strife**s**
roof	roof**s**	belief	belief**s**

There are a few nouns which form their plurals by adding **en** or **ren** to the singular.

Example

ox

ox**<u>en</u>**

child

child**<u>ren</u>**

Besides the above mentioned exceptions, some nouns do not change at all in their plural form.

Example

fish

fish

deer

deer

sheep

sheep

Exercise 6

Fill in the blanks with the ***plurals*** *of the following.*

1\.

one tree

two ________________

2\.

a boy

two ________________

3\.

a cup

three ________________

4\.

a mango

four ________________

5.

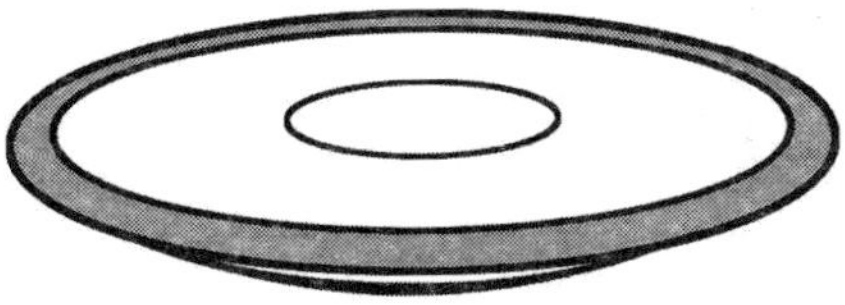

one plate

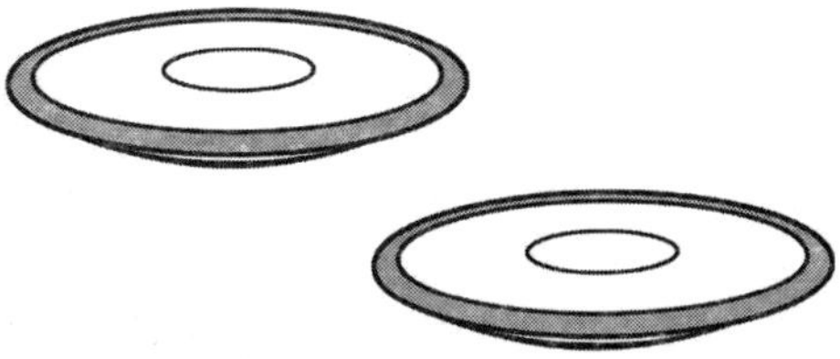

two ______________

6.

one knife

two ______________

7.

one dog

two ______________

8.

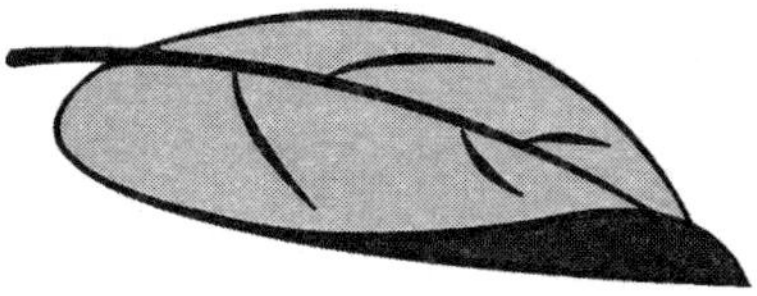

one leaf

many ______________

9.

one watch

two ______________

UNIT 5

NOUNS - GENDER

When nouns denote names of **males**, then they are said to be in the **Masculine Gender**.

When nouns denote names of **females**, then they are said to be in the **Feminine Gender**.

Example

Mrs. Maria | **Rose** | **Henry**

Rose is a girl. She is Mrs. Maria's daughter.
Girl and *daughter* denote ***females***. Hence, they are of the ***feminine gender***.

Henry is a boy. He is Mrs. Maria's son.
Boy and *son* denote ***males***. Hence, they are of the ***masculine gender***.

When nouns denote names of neither **males** nor **females**, then, they are said to be in the **Neuter Gender**.

Example

The baby plays with a ball.

The word *ball* denotes neither **male** nor **female**. Hence, it is in the **neuter gender**.

When nouns denote the names of both **males** and **females**, then they are said to be in the **Common Gender**.

Example

Mr. David and Miss Mary both are teachers. They teach the same class.

The word *teacher* stands for both **male** and **female**. Hence, it is in the **common gender**.

Exercise 1

Pick out the words and place them in the right wagon of the train.

dog	prince	cow	book	grandfather
niece	hen	actress	rock	animal
lion	tree	doctor	tailor	operator
lady	cook	man	mother	emperor
girl	fish	tiger	apple	nephew
water	aunt	cheese	milk	baby
room	bird	pen	teacher	giant
sister				

1. Masculine

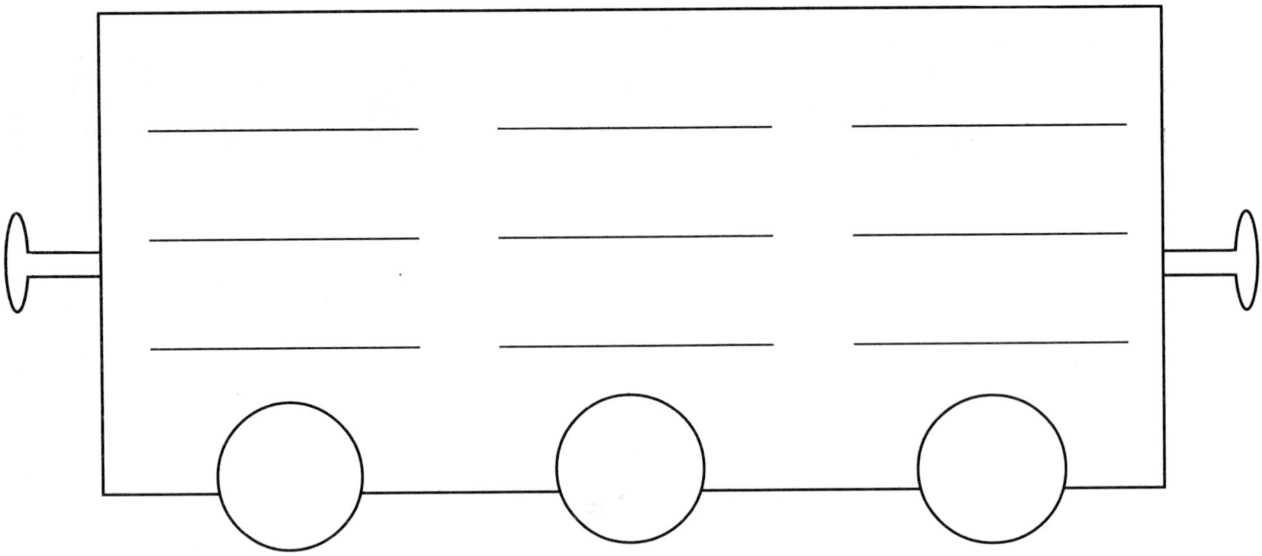

2. Feminine

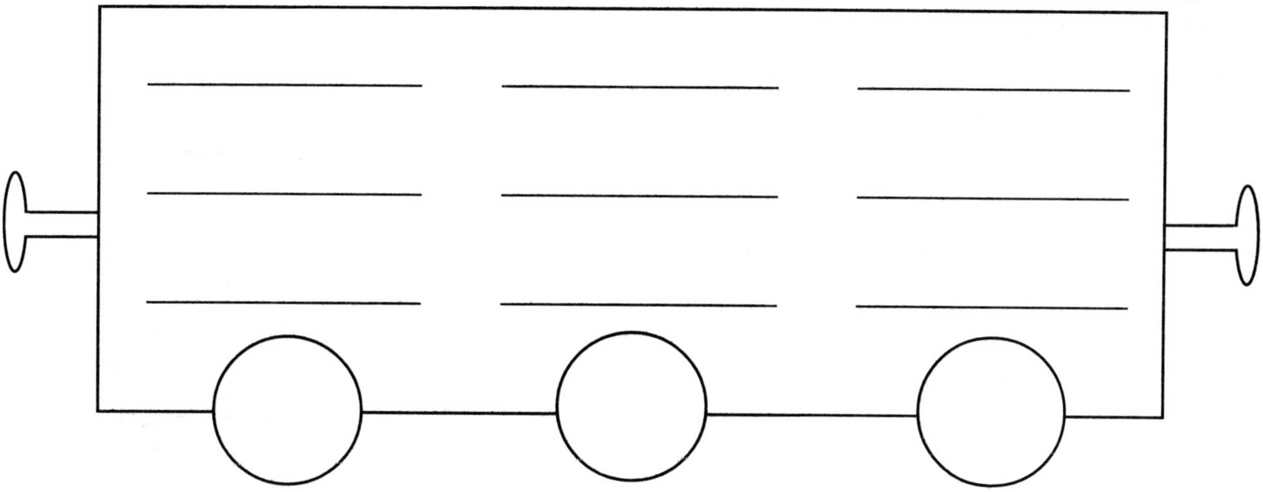

3. Neuter

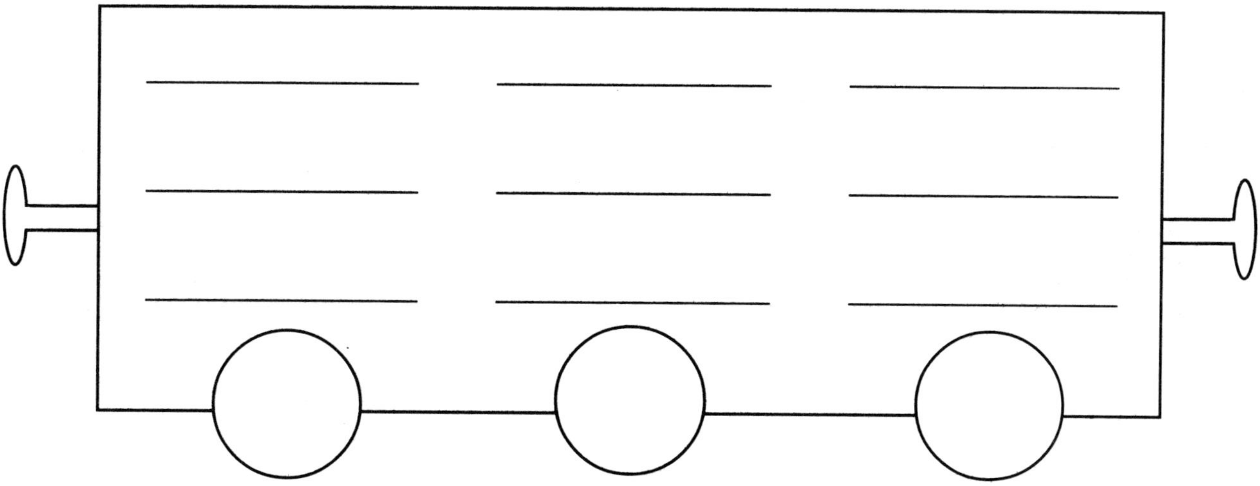

4. Common

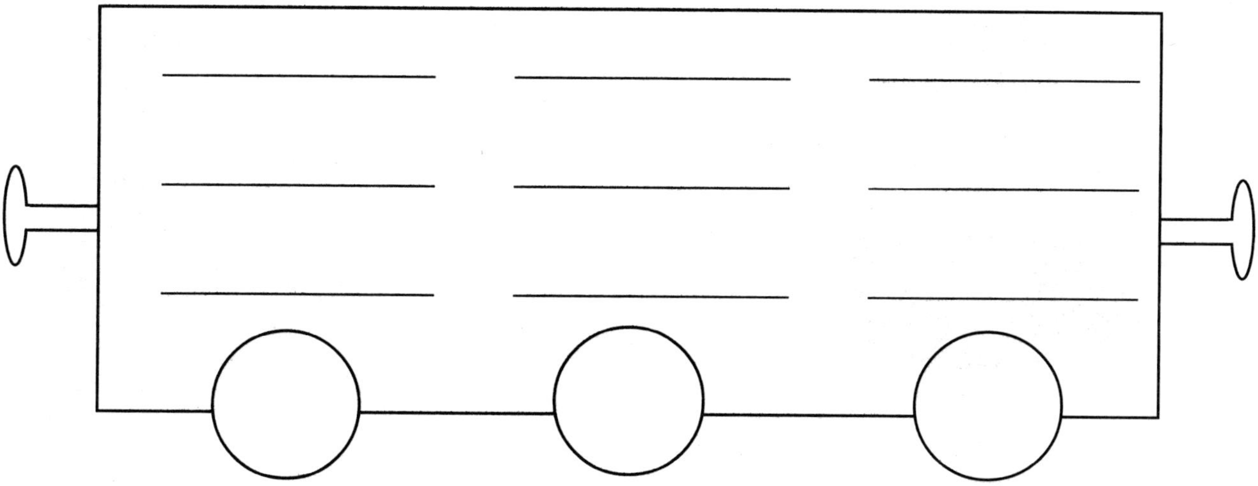

Exercise 2

Fill in the blanks with the correct gender.

Male	***Female***
1. 	
an actor	an ________
2. 	
a cock	a ________
3. 	
a king	a ________

4.

a lion

a ________

5.

uncle

____

6.

son

____

queen	aunt	actress
daughter	hen	lioness

Exercise 3

Supply the missing words.

Male (He - group)	**Female** (She - group)
1. father	____________
2. grandfather	____________
3. nephew	____________
4. sir	____________
5. wizard	____________
6. brother	____________
7. prince	____________
8. waiter	____________
9. husband	____________

Helping Words

wife madam sister

witch niece grandmother

mother waitress princess

UNIT 6

PRONOUNS

Personal Pronouns

A word which is used in place of a noun is a **pronoun**. It helps us in avoiding the repetition of the noun all the time.

Example

John sings a song.
noun

He sings on the stage.
pronoun

Pronoun (singular) I, You, She, He, It

I am a girl.

It is a book.

Exercise 1

Fill in the blanks with 'I', 'She', 'He', 'You', 'It'.

1. ________ am a boy.

2. _________ is a teacher.

3. _________ is a nurse.

4. _________ is a doctor.

5. _________ are Alice!

6. _________ is a wardrobe.

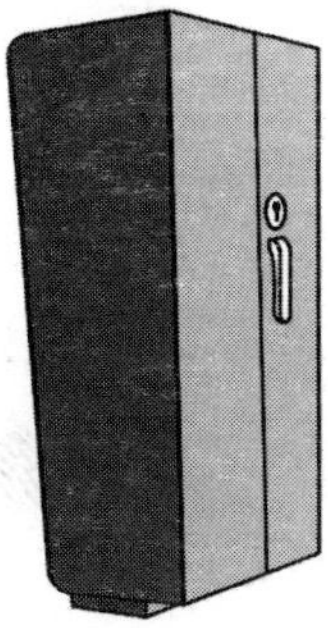

Exercise 2

Fill in the blanks with 'I', 'He', 'She', 'You', 'It'.

1. ________ are a fat boy.

2. ________ is a policeman.

3. ________ is my uncle.

4. ________ is my mother.

5. ________ is a teacher.

6. ________ am Alex.

7. ________ am a pupil.

8. ________ is a bus.

Pronoun (plural) We, You, They

Exercise 3

Fill in the blanks with 'We', 'You', 'They'.

1. 

___________ are pupils.

2.

________ are very naughty boys.

3.

________ are soldiers.

Exercise 4

Fill in the blanks with 'You', 'We', 'They'.

1. I am Kelly. She is Nadia.

   ____________ are friends.

2. Parker, Andy and John are playing in the garden.

   ____________ are all playing in the garden.

3. You are a teacher. Nina is a teacher too.

   ____________ both are teachers.

UNIT 7

VERBS

A **verb** is a doing word. It tells us about an action taking place.

Example

I play football every day.

Jack plays football very well.

Jack is playing football in the ground.

Jack played football yesterday.

Exercise 1

Underline the ***verbs (doing words)*** *in the following sentences.*

1. 

The children play in the sand.

2.

The deer runs fast.

3.

Diana reads her book regularly.

4.

The grocer sells all the necessary things.

5.

David laughs at the clown.

6.

John and Julie walk to school.

7.

Miss Lily teaches English to the class.

8.

The students work hard for the examination.

9.

The girl dances on the stage.

Exercise 2

Choose the correct words from the brackets and underline them.

1. Miss Jane (work, works) hard.

2. The children (play, plays) in the park.

3. Max (fly, flies) a kite in the sky.

4. The singer (sing, sings) well on the stage.

5. The nurses (look, looks) after the patients.

6. Leila (swim, swims) in the pool every day.

7. I (brush, brushes) my teeth every morning.

8. Alex (walk, walks) to school.

9. The pupils (study, studies) in the class.

10. The boys (paint, paints) the picture together.

Exercise 3

Put the correct action word in front of each picture. The words are given below in the box.

1.

____

2.

____

3.

____

4.

____

5.

____

6.

____

7.

____

8.

____

9.

____

10.

____

Helping Words

sing	swim	eat	read
pull	skip	run	dance
	fly	play	

Exercise 4

Circle all the ***doing words****.*

open	big	angry	loud
sweep	wash	heavy	black
dance	tall	bright	sing
heavy	write	fat	read
listen	spoon	speak	radio
John	cry	Danny	play
kick	cake	pull	biscuits
music	enjoy	laugh	night

Exercise 5

Choose the correct word from the box and fill in each blank.

drink	walk	comb	brush
get	put on	eat	wash

A. Every morning I ______________ up at six o'clock. I ______________ my teeth. I ______________ my face. I ______________ my uniform. I ______________ my hair. I ______________ a glass of milk. I ______________ a piece of bread. I ______________ to school.

scatters	comes	plucks
runs	troubles	

B. Everyday a boy ______________ here. He ______________ the flowers and ______________ them. Then he ______________ away. He ______________ the gardener.

UNIT 8

THE VERB – 'TO BE'

Some verbs do not show action. The verbs which tell what some one or something is, are verbs - **to be**.

is, am, are

Singular nouns and pronouns take the singular verb **'is'** except for I and You.

Pronoun I takes the verb **'am'**, while you takes the verb **'are'**.

Plural nouns and pronouns take the plural verb **'are'**.

Example

He **is** a bright boy.

I **am** a student.

They **are** teachers.

She **is** a pretty girl.

The cats **are** hungry.

They **are** my cousins.

Exercise 1

Fill in the blanks with 'is', 'am' or 'are'.

1. 

It __________ a toy.

2. 

The toys __________ beautiful.

3. 

The mango __________ ripe.

4. 

The mangoes ________ ripe.

5. 

She __________ a teacher.

6. 

They __________ teachers.

7. 

I ___________ a student.

8. 

We ___________ students.

9. 

The flower ___________ beautiful.

10. 

The stars _________ bright.

Exercise 2

Choose the correct ***verb - to be*** *to complete these sentences.*

1. John __________ (is, am, are) busy with his friends today.
2. Adam and James __________ (is, am, are) very good friends.
3. I __________ (is, am, are) not John's best friend.
4. Karina __________ (is, am, are) fond of dancing on the stage.
5. Peter __________ (is, am, are) fond of singing on the stage.
6. The children __________ (is, am, are) fond of watching the show.
7. I __________ (is, am, are) happy when I watch the show.
8. They __________ (is, am, are) eager to clap for them.
9. The moon __________ (is, am, are) like a silver disc shining in the sky.
10. The stars __________ (is, am, are) heavenly bodies twinkling in the sky.

Exercise 3

Fill in the blanks with 'am', 'is', or 'are'.

1. Julie __________ dancing.

2. Sara and Miley __________ eating.

3. You __________ very pretty.

4. I __________ doing my homework.

5. The books __________ very useful.

6. The children __________ naughty.

7. The child __________ lovely.

8. I __________ an honest child.

9. The table __________ quite heavy.

10. We __________ students of this school.

11. You __________ very hard working.

12. The lion __________ sleeping.

Exercise 4

Fill in the blanks with 'is', 'am' or 'are'.

I _________ Paul. Sophia _________ my friend. Mary _________ also my friend. Both the girls _________ my neighbours. Sophia _________ living on the second floor. Mary _________ living next door to my house. We always study and play together.

UNIT 9

THE VERB – 'TO HAVE'

Has is used with singular nouns and pronouns.
Have is used with plural nouns and pronouns.
The pronouns 'I' and 'you' take the verb **have**.

Example

The girl **has** curly hair.

The girls **have** curly hair.

Mr. Simon **has** black eyes.

Animals **have** four legs.

I **have** a toy gun.

You **have** a cricket bat.

Exercise 1

*Fill in the blanks with the correct **verb** in the brackets.*

1. I ____________ a new umbrella. (has/have)
2. She ____________ one sister. (has/have)

3. They __________ many books. (has/have)

4. A year __________ 365 days. (has/have)

5. We __________ five books. (has/have)

6. The children __________ gone to the next classroom. (has/have)

7. We __________ two beautiful houses. (has/have)

8. This shop __________ many things. (has/have)

9. I __________ beautiful toys. (has/have)

Exercise 2

Look at the pictures and fill in the blanks with 'has' or 'have'.

1.

I __________ a toy.

2.

You __________ a toy.

3.

We both __________ toys.

4.

He __________ a flower.

5.

She __________ a flower too.

6.

They both __________ flowers.

Exercise 3

Fill in the blanks with ***has*** *or* ***have****.*

(A) Do you __________ a one-pound coin?

(B) Yes, I __________ a one-pound coin.

(C) I __________ to buy a pen. I __________ left my pen at home. Mother __________ gone to market. She __________ locked the house.

(D) We __________ to look for a shop. Do you __________ any shop's address?

(E) Oh dear, I do not __________ any address. I __________ to call my father. Maybe, he can help.

Exercise 4

Fill in the blanks with the words given in the box.

am	is	are	has	have

I ________ Peter. He ________ my brother John.

Tina ________ our little sister.

She ________ a fever today.

She ________ lying in her bed.

Her body ________ not cold but her feet ________ cold.

Tina ________ to rest to get well.

John and I ________ to keep quiet so that we do not disturb Tina.

We cannot play at home.

We ________ to play outside.

But it ________ raining outside.

We ________ to stay inside and play peacefully.

Mother will be angry if we ________ too noisy.

UNIT 10

THE VERB – 'TO DO'

Do or **does** is used to denote when a work is carried out or finished.

In sentences singular nouns and pronouns take the verb **does** except for 'I' and 'you'.

Plural nouns and pronouns take the verb **do**.

'I' and 'you' take the verb **do**.

Example

I **do** a lot of work every day.

He **does** all his home-work.

She **does** her work honestly.

They **do** their work honestly.

Alex **does** swimming well.

Julie **does** painting well.

You **do** your work smartly.

Exercise 1

Look at the pictures and fill in the blanks with 'do' or 'does'.

1. 

The carpenter ________ his work honestly.

2. 

Miss Lily ________ her work cleanly.

3. 

Romeo and Max ________ their jobs smartly.

4. 

Mr. Thomas ________ his work successfully.

5.

_______ the girls dance?

Yes, they __________ .

6.

_______ the birds fly?

Yes, they __________ .

7.

_______ the boy sing?

Yes, he __________ .

8.

_______ the girl swim?

Yes, she __________ .

9.

_______ the dog bark?

Yes, it __________ .

Exercise 2

Make as many sentences as possible from the table given below.

He She	does	
You We I They	do	painting well.

1. He ______________________.

2. She ______________________.

3. You ______________________.

4. We ______________________.

5. I ______________________.

6. They ______________________.

DOING ACTIONS

Example

Mary is **carrying** a basket in her hand.

John is **lighting** a candle.

Jack is **throwing** stones in the water.

Lara is **holding** her father's hand.

Lucy is **chopping** a carrot.

The baby is **drinking** milk.

Exercise 3

Choose the correct word from the box and fill in the blanks:

holding	carrying	drinking	lighting	throwing	chopping

1. Jack is ________________ stones in the water.
2. Daisy is ________________ her father's hand.
3. Mary is ________________ a basket in her hand.
4. The baby is ________________ milk.
5. Jane is ________________ a candle.
6. Lucy is ________________ a carrot.

Exercise 4

Look at the picture and underline the correct doing word.

1. 

Sally is washing the clothes.

2. 

Peter is riding a bicycle.

3. 

John is driving a car.

4. 

The cat is chasing a rat.

5. 

George is watering the plants.

6. 

The grocer is selling rice.

Exercise 5

Choose the correct word from the box and fill in the blanks.

reading	washing	driving	climbing
riding	watering	chasing	selling
walking	drinking		

1. Henry is ______________________ the steps.

2. Mr. David is ______________________ the plants.

3. Mary is ______________________ the clothes.

4. The grocer is ______________________ rice.

5. Sam is ______________________ a bicycle.

6. The lion is ______________________ a deer.

7. I am ______________________ the newspaper.

8. Mrs. Maria is ______________________ a car.

9. Peter is ______________________ the juice.

10. Grandpa is ______________________ in the garden

UNIT 11

TENSES

The **tense** is a form of the **verb** that shows the time of the action.

Present Tense

The action that is taking place **now** is said to be in the Present Tense.

Example

David goes to school **every morning**.

Mother washes clothes on **Saturdays**.

I play cricket **every day**.

Past Tense

The action that has taken place in the **past**, is said to be in the Past Tense.

Example

David went to school **yesterday**.

Mother washed clothes **last Saturday**.

I played cricket **last evening**.

Regular Verb

The **Past Tense** of **regular verbs** is formed by adding **ed** to them.

Example

Present Tense	Past Tense
bark	bark**ed**
play	play**ed**
walk	walk**ed**
open	open**ed**
talk	talk**ed**
work	work**ed**
finish	finish**ed**
knock	knock**ed**

Irregular Verbs

The **Past Tense** of **irregular verbs** is formed by changing the spelling.

Example

Present Tense	Past Tense
write	wr**o**te
see	s**aw**
sleep	sle**pt**
sing	s**a**ng
sit	s**a**t
eat	**ate**
give	g**a**ve
go	**went**

Exercise 1

*Fill in the blanks with the correct **form** of the **verbs**.*

	Present Tense	Past Tense
1.	look	______________
2.	pick	______________
3.	ask	______________
4.	______________	wished
5.	______________	jumped
6.	______________	cried
7.	help	______________
8.	______________	carried
9.	grab	______________
10.	reply	______________

Exercise 2

*Fill in the blanks with the correct **form** of the **verbs**.*

	Present Tense	Past Tense
1.	say	________
2.	make	________
3.	learn	________
4.	________	taught
5.	________	bought
6.	________	made
7.	speak	________
8.	go	________
9.	________	flew
10.	________	got

Exercise 3

Underline the ***verbs*** *in the following sentences and mention the* ***Tenses*** *in the space provided.*

1. She <u>danced</u> in the function last night. Past Tense
2. Annie works in an office in New York. ______________
3. Last year, she went to California. ______________
4. We visit the temple every morning. ______________
5. Alice bought some new dresses yesterday. ______________
6. The little boy drinks milk twice daily. ______________
7. The cat licked all the milk yesterday. ______________

Exercise 4

Fill in the blanks with the correct ***words*** *given in the brackets.*

1. He ____________ us English last year. (teaches, taught)
2. She ____________ a letter to her mother today. (writes, wrote)
3. Tony ____________ over the rope daily. (jumps, jumped)
4. I ____________ a present for my mother on Mothers day. (buy, bought)

5. We ______________ the cartoon show on television last night. (watch, watched)

6. The famous singer ______________ sweetly. (sings, sang)

7. They ______________ home late last night. (reach, reached)

8. The principal ______________ the naughty boys yesterday. (punishes, punished)

Exercise 5

Can you guess the correct form of the words given.

1. Past Tense of **think** ______________
2. Present Tense of **fell** ______________
3. Present Tense of **kicked** ______________
4. Past Tense of **fly** ______________
5. Past Tense of **lend** ______________
6. Present Tense of **crept** ______________
7. Past Tense of **buy** ______________
8. Present Tense of **blew** ______________

UNIT 12

ADJECTIVES

An **adjective** is a word which tells us something more about a <u>noun</u> or a <u>pronoun</u>.

It is a **describing word.**

It tells about the size, shape, colour, amount and much more.

Example

A cat

A <u>black</u> cat

A <u>fat</u> cat

A <u>lazy</u> cat

A girl

A <u>pretty</u> girl

A <u>tall</u> girl

A <u>thin</u> girl

An <u>Indian</u> girl

Exercise 1

Look at the pictures carefully. Underline the correct ***describing words*** *in the brackets.*

1. 

John has a (round, square) box.

2. 

Mother made me a bowl of (cold, hot) soup.

3. 

Mr. Parker is a (fat, thin) man.

4. 

Elephant is a (big, small) animal.

5. 

The (foolish, clever) dog barks at night.

6.

Yesterday was a (sunny, rainy) day.

7.

Max is a (strong, weak) boy.

8.

The cat has a (long, short) tail.

9.

The apples are (white, red) in colour.

10.

We must wear (cotton, woollen) dress in winter.

Exercise 2

*Pick out the **adjectives** from the following sentences together with the **nouns**, they describe.*

	adjective	noun
1. Peter is a naughty boy.		
2. Tina is a little girl.		
3. Mrs. Maria is a kind lady.		
4. The big cat ran after the mouse.		
5. The Taj Mahal is a beautiful building.		
6. Penguins love to live in cooler places.		
7. The large elephant is a good friend of Andy.		
8. The children wear red uniforms.		
9. Mary likes a strawberry cake.		
10. Lily has many books in her bag.		

Exercise 3

*Describe the pictures. Use as many **adjectives** as you can.*

1. 

A pretty doll.
A ______________ doll.
A ______________ doll.

2. 

A black dog.
A ______________ dog.
A ______________ dog.

3. 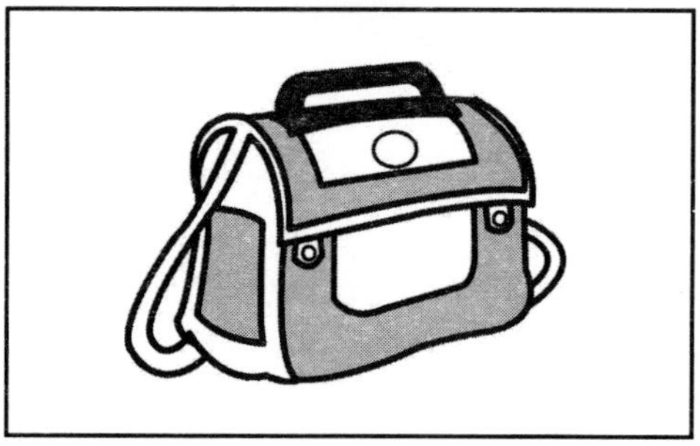

A white bag.
A ______________ bag.
A ______________ bag.

4. 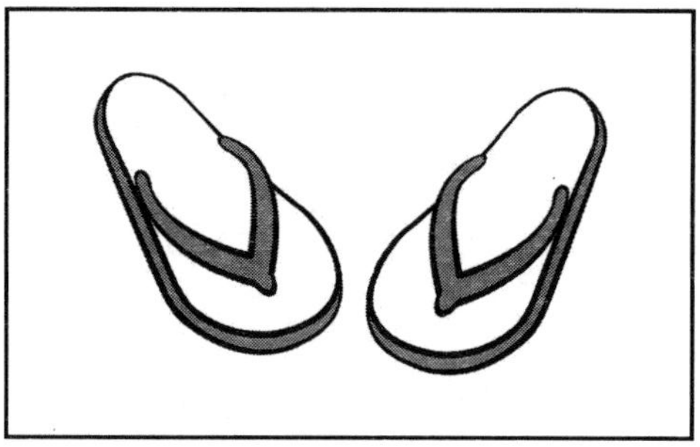

A pair of comfortable slippers.
A pair of ______________ slippers.
A pair of ______________ slippers.

5. 

A brown bear.
A ______________ bear.
A ______________ bear.

6.

The juicy apples.
The ____________ apples.
The ____________ apples.

7.

A brown cat.
A ____________ cat.
A ____________ cat.

8.

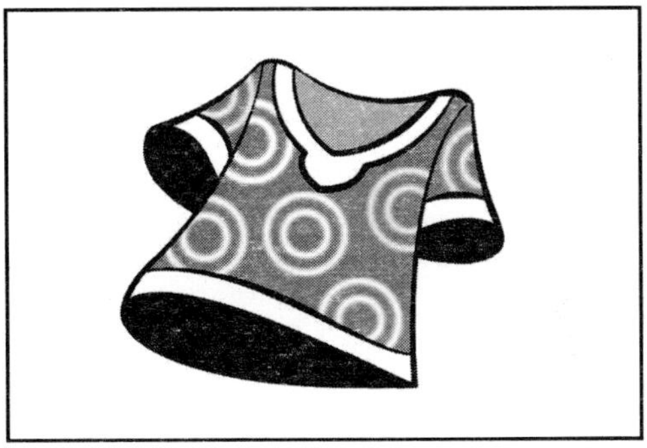

A new dress.
A ____________ dress.
A ____________ dress.

Helping Words

toy	red	soft	big
rubber	small	beautiful	happy
teddy	paper	fresh	fat
new	wooden	lazy	school

Note : An adjective may come before a noun, after a noun or after a linking verb i.e. **is, are**.

Example

The book is **heavy**.

The dogs are **playful**.

Exercise 4

*Put the **adjectives** before the **nouns**.*

1. The boys are happy.  ____________________

2. The sun is bright.  ____________________

3. The day is cloudy. 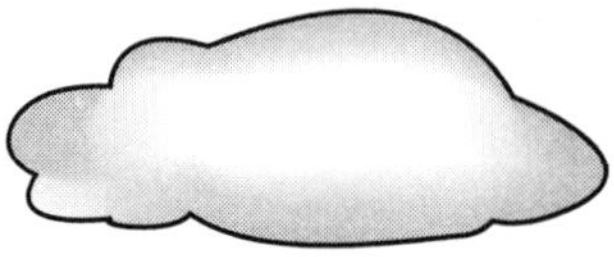 ____________________

4. The pair of shoes is old.  ____________________

5. The cake is sweet.  ____________________

6. The paint is wet.  ____________________

Exercise 5

*Match the **adjectives** in column A to their right pairs in column B.*

A.	**Column**	**B. Column**
1.	clear	knife 
2.	clever	jewellery 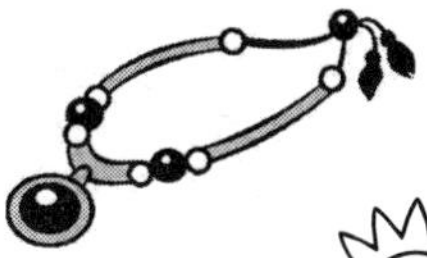
3.	sharp	day 
4.	hot	grapes 
5.	diamond	pillow 
6.	rainy	fox 
7.	pretty	businessman 
8.	soft	girl 
9.	rich	soup 
10.	green	water 

UNIT 13

COMMON VOCABULARY

Parts of My Body

I see with my **eyes**.

I smell with my **nose**.

I eat with my **mouth**.

I clap with my **hands**.

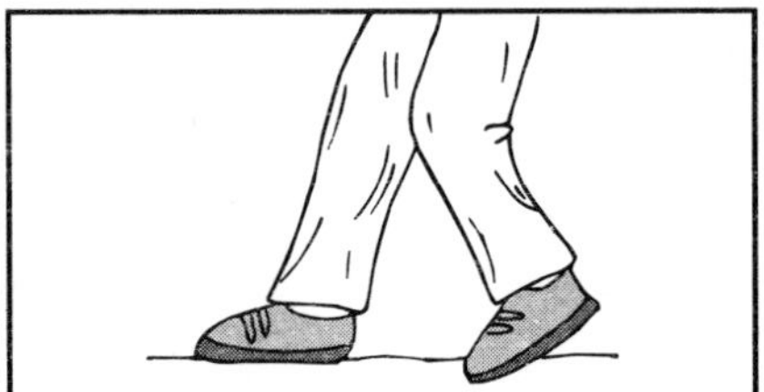

I walk with my **legs**.

I hear with my **ears**.

Exercise 1

Write True (T) or False (F).

1. I walk with my hands. (   )
2. I eat with my mouth. (   )
3. I smell with my nose. (   )
4. I hear with my eyes. (   )
5. I clap with my ears. (   )
6. I see with my eyes. (   )

Exercise 2

Rearrange the jumbled words and write the sentences correctly.

1. my I eat mouth with. ____________________
2. eyes my I see with. ____________________
3. with I walk legs my. ____________________
4. clap hands I my with. ____________________
5. my with hear I ears. ____________________

Exercise 3

Match them up.

Racket

Jam

Nest

Ball

Bread

Bird

Teacher

Nurse

Doctor

Chair

Table

Blackboard

Cow

Clouds

Rain

Milk

Exercise 4

Choose the correct letter from the bracket to complete the word.

1. Br ___ ad (a, e, o)
2. Ne ___ t (s, t, r)
3. Rai ___ (p, n, s)
4. Nur ____ e (r, s, i)
5. T ___ ble (b, a, e)
6. Clo ___ ds (p, u, s)

FRUITS

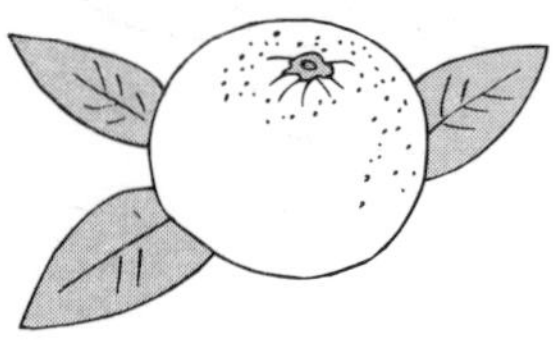

Orange

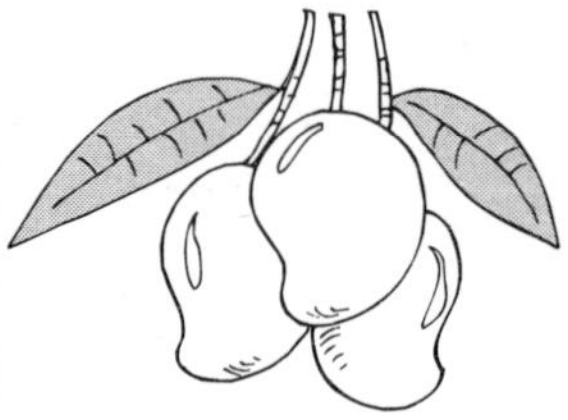

Mangoes

Pineapple

Bananas

Peach

Grapes

Apple

Pear

VEGETABLES

Tomato

Potato

Carrot

Onion

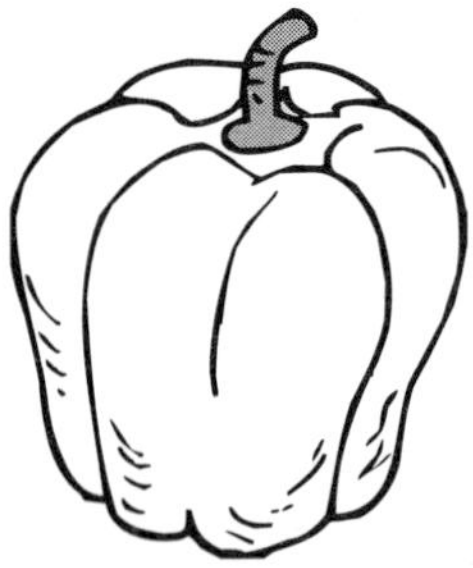

Capsicum

Cauliflower

Radish

Pumpkin

Exercise 5

Write True (T) or False (F).

1. Apple is a vegetable. ( )
2. Carrot is a fruit. ( )
3. Banana is a fruit. ( )
4. Mango is a vegetable. ( )
5. Orange is a fruit. ( )
6. Cabbage is a fruit. ( )
7. Peach is a fruit. ( )
8. Onion is a vegetable. ( )

SOUNDS OF ANIMALS

A dog **barks**.

A tiger **growls**.

A lion **roars**.

A wolf **howls**.

An elephant **trumpets**.

A cat **mews**.

Exercise 6

Match the animals with the sounds.

1.	An elephant	a)	barks
2.	A cat	b)	roars
3.	A lion	c)	howls
4.	A wolf	d)	growls
5.	A dog	e)	trumpets
6.	A tiger	f)	mews

HOMES OF ANIMALS

A rat lives in a **hole**.

A bear lives in a **cave**.

A rabbit lives in a **burrow**.

A bird lives in a **nest**.

A lion lives in a **den**.

A cow lives in a **shed**.

A fish lives in **water**.

A dog lives in a **kennel**.

A horse lives in a **stable**.

Exercise 7

Write True (T) or False (F).

1. A dog lives in a burrow. (   )
2. A fish lives in water. (   )
3. A rat lives in a den. (   )

4. A bear lives in a cave. ( )
5. A rabbit lives in a stable. ( )
6. A cow lives in a kennel. ( )
7. A bird lives in a nest. ( )
8. A lion does not live in a den. ( )

Exercise 8

Match the animals with their homes.

1.	Bear	a)	Den
2.	Fish	b)	Stable
3.	Rabbit	c)	Kennel
4.	Lion	d)	Nest
5.	Rat	e)	Burrow
6.	Horse	f)	Water
7.	Dog	g)	Shed
8.	Cow	h)	Cave
9.	Bird	i)	Hole

Exercise 9

Rearrange the jumbled letters and write the words correctly.

1. bitrab

____

2. sbleta

____

3. hrseo

____

4. rowbur

____

5. wtera

____

6. nelken

____

UNIT 14

READING SKILLS

READING COMPREHENSION - I

Good Habits

Wake up early.

Brush your teeth twice a day.

Take a bath every day.

Wear clean clothes.

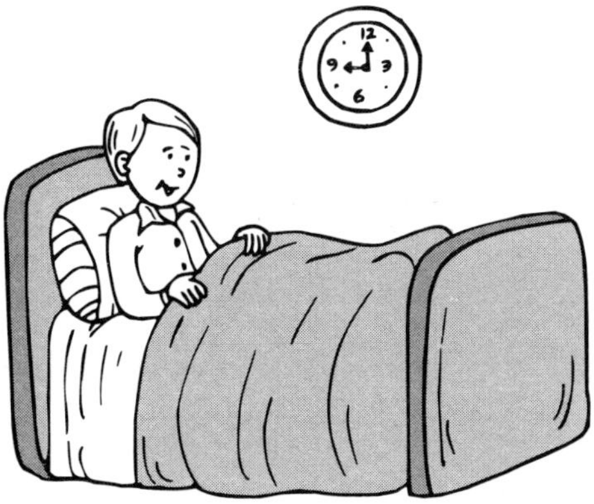

Go to sleep early.

Show respect to elders.

Say "Sorry" when you do something wrong.

Say "Thank you" when you receive a gift.

Exercise 1

Strike out (×) the incorrect option.

1. Wake up
   a) early b) late
2. Brush your teeth
   a) twice a week b) twice a day
3. Go to sleep
   a) late b) early
4. Show respect to
   a) elders b) thieves

READING COMPREHENSION - II

Who Am I ?

Exercise 2

Tick (✓) the correct option.

1. I am very huge.
   My ears are very big.
   I have a trunk.

   (a) Cow ☐ (b) Elephant ☐

   (c) Dog ☐ (d) Cat ☐

2. I am beautiful.
I have seven colours.
You can see me in the sky.

(a) Clouds ☐ (b) Rainbow ☐
(c) Sun ☐ (d) Moon ☐

3. I am small.
I have a bushy tail.
I like carrots.

(a) Dog ☐ (b) Cat ☐
(c) Rabbit ☐ (d) Cow ☐

4. I have two colourful wings.
I sit on the flowers.
I drink honey.

(a) Ant ☐ (b) Crow ☐
(c) Butterfly ☐ (d) Grasshopper ☐

READING COMPREHENSION - III
Asking Questions

How old are you?
I am five years old.

How do you go to school?

I go to school by bus.

What is your favourite food?

My favourite food is noodles.

What time do you go to bed?

I go to bed at eight o'clock.

Exercise 3

Circle the correct spelling.

1.	(a)	yaers	(b)	years
2.	(a)	scoohl	(b)	school
3.	(a)	favourite	(b)	favuorite
4.	(a)	noodels	(b)	noodles
5.	(a)	waht	(b)	what
6.	(a)	time	(b)	tiem
7.	(a)	eihgt	(b)	eight

PICTURE COMPREHENSION - IV

Exercise 4

Look at the picture carefully.
Fill in the blanks by giving the right answers to the questions given below.

1. What is there in the picture?
2. What kind of animal is it?
3. How many legs has it?
4. What kind of trunk has it?
5. Is it an intelligent animal?
6. How is it useful to man?
7. What are its teeth called?
8. Is it a faithful animal?
9. Where did you see it?
10. How do you like it?

four	tusks	large	intelligent	elephant
very	zoo	faithful	cylindrical	hunting

It is an 1 ________________. It is a 2 ________________ animal. It has 3 ________________ legs. It has a 4 ________________ trunk. It is an 5 ________________ animal. It is used for 6 ________________ tigers. Its teeth are called 7 ________________. It is a 8 ________________ animal. I saw it in a 9 ________________. I like it 10 ________________ much.

PICTURE COMPREHENSION - V

Exercise 5

Look at the picture carefully.
Fill in the blanks by giving the right answers to the questions given below.

1. What is this?
2. How many legs has a chair?
3. Name two other parts of the chair.
4. What is the chair made of?
5. Who made it?
6. For how much did you buy it?
7. From where did you buy it?
8. How do you use it?
9. Is it a big chair or small one?
10. How do you like it?

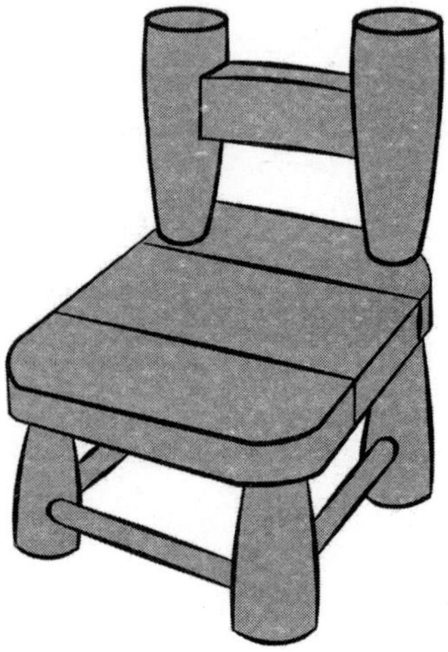

back	small	wood	$20	seat	sit
four	very	furniture	chair	carpenter	

This is a 1 ____________ . It has 2 ____________ legs. Two other parts of the chair are the 3 ____________ and the 4 ____________. The chair is made of 5 ____________ . A 6 ____________ made it. I bought it for 7 ____________. I bought it from the 8 ____________ shop. I 9 ____________ on it along with my doll. It is a 10 ____________ chair. I like it 11 ____________ much.

READING COMPREHENSION - VI

My Pet Dog

I have a dog at home. His name is Rocky. He is an intelligent dog. He wags his tail when he sees my father. He barks at strangers. I love my dog very much.

Exercise 6

Rearrange the jumbled letters.

1. mena __________
2. fehtar __________
3. heom __________
4. Ryokc __________
5. rabks __________
6. ryve __________
7. inlteligten __________
8. trsanrsge __________

STORIES OF VALUES

I. A Thirsty Crow

Once upon a time a crow was very thirsty. He was flying here and there in search of water. Suddenly, he saw a pitcher of water in a garden. He sat down on the edge of the pitcher and looked down into it. The water level was very low in it. His beak could not reach the water. He hit upon a plan. He picked up small pebbles lying on the ground and dropped them one by one into the pitcher. The water level in the pitcher rose up. Soon it was within his reach. He drank the water and flew away.

Moral : Where there is a will, there is a way.

Exercise 7

1. What for was the crow flying here and there?

____

2. What did the crow pick up from the ground?

____

II. A Selfish Friend

Once upon a time, two friends were going through a thick forest. They promised to help each other at the time of need. Suddenly they saw a bear coming towards them. One of the friends at once climbed up a tree to save his life. The other one did not know how to climb up a tree. He was helpless. He lay down on the ground and pretended to be dead. The bear sniffed him and went away taking him to be dead. The selfish friend climbed down the tree and said, "What did the bear say in your ear?" The boy answered that the bear had advised him to beware of false and selfish friends.

Moral : A friend in need is a friend indeed.

Exercise 8

1. Whom did the two friends see coming towards them?

____

____

2. Why did one of the friends lie down on the ground?

____

____

ENRICH YOUR GRAMMAR PRIMARY ONE

ANSWERS

Unit 1 (Page 5)

Exercise 1

1. ☑ 2. ☒
3. ☑ 4. ☑
5. ☑ 6. ☒
7. ☑ 8. ☑
9. ☒

Exercise 2
1. The little boy rode his bicycle.
2. It rained throughout the day.
3. The class was over by nine o'clock.
4. The little girl played with her doll.
5. John is fond of chocolates.
6. Mary loves to eat ice-cream.
7. The girl won the first prize.

Unit 2 (Page 7)

Exercise 1
1. flower 2. bird
3. apple 4. church
5. postman 6. moon
7. horse 8. book
9. radio 10. aeroplane

Exercise 2

Persons:
girl, Diana, man, baby, policeman.
Places:
church, Taj Mahal, hospital, island, London
Animals:
dog, cat, cow, tiger, bear
Things:
car, water, clothes, leaf, flower

Exercise 3

A.
1. Daisy 2. Mary
3. John 4. Alex
5. Peter 6. David

B.
1. Eiffel Tower 2. Taj Mahal
3. Nigeria 4. bird park
5. Supermarket 6. zoo

C.
1. cow 2. dog
3. hen 4. lion
5. peacock 6. horse

D.
1. pencil box 2. lunch box
3. text books 4. note books
5. ruler 6. pen

E.
1. Henry 2. Karina
3. Sophia 4. Simon
5. Ruby 6. Johnny

F.
1. rice 2. bread
3. noodles 4. ice-cream
5. hamburger 6. boiled eggs

Exercise 4

Johnny, woman, Paris,
book, rose, ribbon,
mangoes, sky, star,
moon, school, park,
train, hospital

Exercise 5
1. Lily, dress
2. horse, stable
3. Nile, river, world
4. Peter, balls
5. man, boy
6. Maria, clothes, day
7. Daisy, newspaper
8. students, bus

Exercise 6
1. loves 2. brings
3. eat 4. sing
5. sit

Exercise 7
1. park 2. boys
3. girl 4. tree
5. flowers 6. ducks
7. pond 8. ball
9. swing 10. grass

Exercise 8

1. tailor
2. cobbler
3. teacher
4. barber
5. postman
6. washerman
7. nurse
8. painter
9. carpenter
10. pilot
11. grocer
12. milkman

Exercise 9

1. boy
2. bird
3. girl
4. teacher
5. boys
6. lady
7. dog
8. moon

Unit 3 (Page 18)

Exercise 1

1. cars
2. dogs
3. apples
4. eggs
5. girls
6. horses
7. bottles
8. chairs
9. boys

Exercise 2

A.

There are one pen, two pencils, one ruler and two erasers.

B.

She has three apples, two pomegranates, four mangoes and one pineapple.

Exercise 3

1. ducks
2. swans
3. peacocks
4. crow
5. hens
6. parrots

Exercise 4

1. dolls, balls
2. teddy bear, cars
3. aeroplanes, ship
4. cats, dog
5. guns

Unit 4 (Page 24)

Exercise 1

1. ladies
2. berries
3. butterflies
4. candies
5. flies

Exercise 2

1. days
2. rays
3. donkeys
4. toys
5. trays

Exercise 3

1. mangoes
2. buffaloes
3. heroes
4. potatoes
5. mosquitoes

Exercise 4

1. lives
2. wives
3. calves

Exercise 5

1. geese
2. women
3. mice
4. feet
5. teeth

Exercise 6

1. trees
2. boys
3. cups
4. mangoes
5. plates
6. knives
7. dogs
8. leaves
9. watches

Unit 5 (Page 32)

Exercise 1

1. **Masculine**:
   dog, lion, prince, man
   tiger, giant, grandfather,
   emperor, nephew
2. **Feminine**:
   niece, lady, girl, hen,
   aunt, cow, actress,
   mother, sister
3. **Neuter**:
   water, tree, pen, cheese,
   book, rock, apple, milk,
   room
4. **Common**:
   bird, cook, fish, doctor, teacher,
   tailor, animal, operator, baby

Exercise 2

1. actress
2. hen
3. queen
4. lioness
5. aunt
6. daughter

Exercise 3

1. mother
2. grandmother
3. niece
4. madam
5. witch
6. sister
7. princess
8. waitress
9. wife

Unit 6 (Page 39)

Exercise 1

1. I
2. She
3. She
4. He
5. You
6. It

Exercise 2

1. You
2. He
3. He
4. She
5. He/She
6. I
7. I
8. It

Exercise 3

1. We
2. You
3. They

Exercise 4

1. We
2. They
3. You

Unit 7 (Page 44)

Exercise 1

1. play
2. runs
3. reads
4. sells
5. laughs
6. walk
7. teaches
8. work
9. dances

Exercise 2

1. works
2. play
3. flies
4. sings
5. look
6. swims
7. brush
8. walks
9. study
10. paint

Exercise 3

1. skip
2. dance
3. fly
4. kick
5. read
6. pull
7. run
8. eat
9. swim
10. sing

Exercise 4

open,	sweep,	wash,
dance,	sing,	write,
read,	listen,	speak,
cry,	play,	kick,
pull,	enjoy,	laugh

Exercise 5

A. Every morning I get up at six o'clock. I brush my teeth. I wash my face. I put on my uniform. I comb my hair. I drink a glass of milk. I eat a piece of bread. I walk to school.

B. Everyday a boy comes here. He plucks the flowers and scatters them. Then he runs away. He troubles the gardener.

Unit 8 (Page 51)

Exercise 1

1. is
2. are
3. is
4. are
5. is
6. are
7. am
8. are
9. is
10. are

Exercise 2

1. is
2. are
3. am
4. is
5. is
6. are
7. am
8. are
9. is
10. are

Exercise 3

1. is
2. are
3. are
4. am
5. are
6. are
7. is
8. am
9. is
10. are
11. are
12. is

Exercise 4

I am Paul. Sophia is my friend. Mary is also my friend. Both the girls are my neighbours. Sophia is living on second floor. Mary is living next door to my house. We always study and play together.

Unit 9 (Page 56)

Exercise 1

1. have
2. has
3. have
4. has
5. have
6. have
7. have
8. has
9. have

Exercise 2

1. have
2. have
3. have
4. has
5. has
6. have

Exercise 3

(A) have

(B) have

(C) have, have, has, has (D) have, have
(E) have, have

Exercise 4

I <u>am</u> Peter. He <u>is</u> my brother John. Tina <u>is</u> our little sister. She <u>has</u> a fever today. She <u>is</u> lying in her bed. Her body <u>is</u> not cold but her feet <u>are</u> cold. Tina <u>has</u> to rest to get well. John and I <u>have</u> to keep quiet so that we do not disturb Tina. We cannot play at home. We <u>have</u> to play outside. But it <u>is</u> raining outside. We <u>have</u> to stay at inside and play peacefully. Mother will be angry if we <u>are</u> too noisy.

Unit 10 (Page 61)

Exercise 1

1. does
2. does
3. do
4. does
5. Do, do
6. Do, do
7. Does, does
8. Does, does
9. Does, does

Exercise 2

1. He does painting well.
2. She does painting well.
3. You do painting well.
4. We do painting well.
5. I do painting well.
6. They do painting well.

Exercise 3

1. throwing
2. holding
3. carrying
4. drinking
5. lighting
6. chopping

Exercise 4

1. <u>washing</u>
2. <u>riding</u>
3. <u>driving</u>
4. <u>chasing</u>
5. <u>watering</u>
6. <u>selling</u>

Exercise 5

1. climbing
2. watering
3. washing
4. selling
5. riding
6. chasing
7. reading
8. driving
9. drinking
10. walking

Unit 11 (Page 68)

Exercise 1

1. looked
2. picked
3. asked
4. wish
5. jump
6. cry
7. helped
8. carry
9. grabbed
10. replied

Exercise 2

1. said
2. made
3. learnt/learned
4. teach
5. buy
6. make
7. spoke
8. went
9. fly
10. get

Exercise 3

1. <u>danced</u> Past Tense
2. <u>works</u> Present Tense
3. <u>went</u> Past Tense
4. <u>visit</u> Present Tense
5. <u>bought</u> Past Tense
6. <u>drinks</u> Present Tense
7. <u>licked</u> Past Tense

Exercise 4

1. taught
2. wrote
3. jumps
4. bought
5. watched
6. sings
7. reached
8. punished

Exercise 5

1. thought
2. fall
3. kick
4. flew
5. lent
6. creep
7. bought
8. blow

Unit 12 (Page 74)

Exercise 1

1. round
2. hot
3. fat
4. big
5. clever
6. rainy
7. strong
8. long
9. red
10. woollen

Exercise 2

1. naughty-boy
2. little-girl
3. kind-lady
4. big-cat
5. beautiful-building
6. cooler-places
7. large-elephant, good-friend
8. red-uniforms
9. strawberry-cake
10. many-books

Exercise 3

1. wooden, new
2. small, happy
3. school, paper
4. big, rubber
5. teddy, toy
6. red, fresh
7. fat, lazy
8. beautiful, soft

Exercise 4

1. happy boys	2. bright sun
3. cloudy day	4. old shoes
5. sweet cake	6. wet paint

Exercise 5

1. clear-water	2. clever-fox
3. sharp-knife	4. hot-soup
5. diamond-jewellery	6. rainy-day
7. pretty-girl	8. soft-pillow
9. rich-businessman	10. green-grapes

Unit 13 (Page 82)

Exercise 1

1. F	2. T	3. T	4. F
5. F	6. T		

Exercise 2

1. I eat with my mouth.
2. I see with my eyes.
3. I walk with my legs.
4. I clap with my hands.
5. I hear with my ears.

Exercise 3

Racket - Ball	Nest - Bird
Bread - Jam	Teacher - Blackboard
Doctor - Nurse	Table - Chair
cow - milk	rain - clouds

Exercise 4

1. Bread	2. Nest	3. Rain
4. Nurse	5. Table	6. Clouds

Exercise 5

1. (F)	2. (F)	3. (T)	4. (F)
5. (T)	6. (F)	7. (T)	8. (T)

Exercise 6

1. e	2. f	3. b	4. c
5. a	6. d		

Exercise 7

1. (F)	2. (T)	3. (F)	4. (T)
5. (F)	6. (F)	7. (T)	8. (F)

Exercise 8

1. h	2. f	3. e	4. a
5. i	6. b	7. c	8. g
9. d			

Exercise 9

1. rabbit	2. stable	3. horse
4. burrow	5. water	6. kennel

Unit 14 (Page 91)

Exercise 1

1. b	2. a	3. a	4. b

Exercise 2

1. b	2. b	3. c	4. c

Exercise 3

1. b	2. b	3. a	4. b
5. b	6. a	7. b	

Exercise 4

1. elephant	2. large
3. four	4. cylindrical
5. intelligent	6. hunting
7. tusks	8. faithful
9. zoo	10. very

Exercise 5

1. chair	2. four	3. seat
4. back	5. wood	6. carpenter
7. $ 20	8. furniture	9. sit
10. small	11. very	

Exercise 6

1. name	2. father	3. home
4. Rocky	5. barks	6. very
7. intelligent	8. strangers	

Exercise 7

1. The crow was flying here and there in search of water.
2. He picked up small pebbles lying on the ground.

Exercise 8

1. The two friends saw a bear coming towards them.
2. He lay down on the ground and pretended to be dead.